"Poetry that takes you by the hand and leads you into the woods"

FAWN PRESS

Elements: Natural & The Supernatural

This edition published in 2021 by Fawn Press.

Cover design by Fawn Press.

ISBN 978-1-3999-0449-0

Printed and bound by Kingate Press, Birmingham, UK.

Contents
Foreward by Scarlett Ward-Bennett

Foreward

You hold in your hands our debut publication - we're very excited to meet you, dear Reader!

When I first envisioned an anthology to debut Fawn Press, I knew I wanted it to be something of a celebration of the natural world. The press was born from the heart of Staffordshire, a place which, thanks to its geographical positioning between the great Cannock Chase Forest, and the bigger towns and cities of the Black Country, is unusual and unique in its relationship between nature and urban; the natural and the man-made. On the fringe of city life, yet deeply influenced by forests, farmland, fields and hedgerows, I knew I wanted our first theme to reflect the diverse identity of The Creative County, as we invited Poets from much further afield to share their experience of the natural and supernatural elements that make up this world.

The Elements as a theme arose when I was considering what would be open enough to invite creative interpretation, whilst still steering a topic. When submissions opened, I predicted that our inbox was going to be crammed with Eco poetry, and whilst there is certainly a good deal of excellent poems of that kind in this anthology, it quickly became apparent that our relationship with our environment is so drenched in our day to day living, that the submissions we received explored the deep and complex relationship between the natural world and our own, in intimate and sensitive ways, beyond simply *the climate*.

So often, when we tell stories about our environment, so too do we reveal parts of ourselves, our experience as humans, and the deep connections between one another. These wonderful poems selected and assorted for you in this book harmonise and chime with one another in such a way that will celebrate, illuminate, and connect. They traverse the vocabulary available to us to explore our universe, and the realms beyond it.

From the molecular chaos of running water and the impatient budding of leaves in Spring, to the whispering aether that fills the darkness of night, I will leave you now in the capable hands of our spectacular Poets.

Scarlett Ward-Bennett - Founder & Editor

5

On an English Apple

I hold the orb of England
in the palm of my still fleshy
hand, unsullied by a callus
or a cut or disappointment:
tapered fingers curled round this
scarred and severed fruit of Eden,
contours of subdued vermilion
with nostalgic pink and ochre,
tainted by a jealous splotch of
brown, elsewhere a tender skin spot
large enough to fit my thumbprint.

Underneath the spots the tangy
blood of Nature's meanest daughter,
plucked by me, her newest mistress,
from a basket of her sisters,
from the womb of Holborn market,
brought out through a plastic exit
into merciless December;
my tongue's ten thousand citizens
rejoice in their discovery—
unadulterated sweetness
in a swollen, smoggy city
and for one delicious instant
I have known a day in Eden.

Cecilia M. Gigliotti

Sonnet 3: On Late Nights

To burn the midnight oil's a practice meant
To warm the winter of our discontent,
And yet seldom produces such a spark
As brightens any outlook, save the dark
Of physically vacant village streets.
'Tis at this hour the supernatural meets
The world of men, their forms of dormant clay
Susceptible to otherworldly play:
All hollow vessels, ripened for possession
And varied ghostly manners of expression—
All prone, all vulnerable, but the one
Who cranes and pushes pen 'til she is done
And prays the Sandman rest for her contrive,
Deepest oblivion—if he'll arrive.

Cecilia M. Gigliotti

The Lady of the Forest

The Lady of the Forest sleeps under a mound of moss, behind a shivering curtain of bracken. She is surrounded by the splintered limbs of trees: a wooden boneyard, where the slow strum of crickets comfort the dying shrubs, shrivelling in Autumn.

Some say she has slept for a thousand years. She rooted herself to the safest place she could find, biding her time; as she slept, her limbs grew into thick, choking vines, fattened on the dead-rich soil. They tighten their misguided grip on her as she sleeps; a languid, voluptuous suffocation.

She is diminished. Forgotten. Trapped in a myth. Her eyes have become the birthplace of spiderlings, dark sockets glittering with tiny, translucent arachnids. A parade of black ants draws a smile from ear to wooden ear, marching across the bark of her lips. She dreams of tearing her mouth open, pulling the creatures from the unwilling incubator of her body, from the cavernous knot where her heart used to beat. She longs for the courage to burst from her mossy hovel, to announce her reckoning, but

she waits, and draws a shallow, rattling breath.

Roz Turner

Truffles

The door breathes calmly – in, out,
bends its frame against the hinge's grip.
I am seeing the world through a crystal ball.

That's interesting. I curl into you
and my hands soften into blunted paws.
My tail relaxes into a small 'c' under the rose-gold light.

A band of warmth shudders through my body;
it starts around my ankles, grows thicker at the knee.
By the time it reaches my chest it burns,

but I stay the course. The sofa bobs like a boat.
I sink deeper into a blanket of prismatic light,
letting the woollen ocean waves roll

and rise over my growing disquiet.
The door flexes again. Silent. This new world
is leaking away, dripping at the seams

with acidic efficiency, melting the vivid scales
from my eyes, collecting in my stomach.
My breath

is evaporated poison, constructed from the forest floor:
the last laugh of a thousand dead and rotten things
cursing their way through my blood.

Roz Turner

Collapse at St Mary's Churchyard, Whitby

Today, the beach is choked with coffins:
a shipwreck circled by shrieking gulls.

Last night, the land slipped:
pulled a cliff over itself,
retreated further into its molten belly.
The dead went tumbling after.

Meanwhile, the ghost of Captain William Scoresby
scries the coast with a gossamer telescope
from the crow's nest of an ethereal ship.
His phantom crew hoist delicate, shifting sails

as they prepare to return, under billowing silk,
to the pile of dark debris;
to claim their bodies
from the slip of the land.

The dead will rise as mist in the wind,
atomising in the unsavoury air.

Roz Turner

The Wolf-Bride

To the thud of drum and the spill of wine
from skins she is carried at midwinter
to her wedding in the wood.

A pretty girl who won't marry is a lit fuse
and the Wolf-King is always hungry;
a deal was struck and no matter how hard

mother sobbed, the white dress was stitched tight,
a trousseau packed with meaty bones by whispering
aunts. Now strangers offer amulets in waxed paper —

wolf teeth, bone-pearls, carved wings for the afterlife.
She is smiling more than anyone would like.
Better a wolf than a man for a husband, she tells them.

Better a wolf who knows the joy
of loping beneath snow laden trees
than your yoke of slops and pans.

Mother, she says, don't cry, she would rather bear
wolf-cubs; prefers their bark and suckle
to the long cling of a human child.

The drums fall silent as she reaches the clearing
where a seal fat fire burns
under the opal moon; the Wolf-King turns

to behold his reward for eating nothing
but starved beasts when the snows rise like white loaves.
She stares back at his yellow teeth and eyes,

the fur bursting from his neck-tie,
then at the crown waiting for her on the altar.
She holds out her hand for him to kiss, or bite.

Charlotte Baldwin

Wheel Of Deer

Anxiety is common in prey animals

**Safety is a woodland pool with
a flat surface.** It is a moment she
may witness once in her lifetime
and know only by a slight change
in her breathing.

Hesitation is a dance of raised hoof and
twitching ear. She will be a slave to this
choreography all her life; it will haunt the
handful of dreams she tumbles into.

Deer do not accept gifts. You may lay before
her your life, dipped in honey, and she will not
lick it because it bears the unmistakable stench of
your fingerprints.

Running is the only prayer she knows. Running is
plea. Running is praise. Running is all her body would
give up if she were turned inside out by a fox.

**Escape is a tunnel
entered at birth.**
Shadows of pursuers
stretch, shrink across its
walls. She runs, but the
circle of freedom
dangling ahead never
grows any closer.

No one can sing a deer to sleep because a
deer can never fully understand what sleep is.
Where sleep is the absence of fear, you
weight one end of her existence; the total
number of eyeballs watching her every
movement weights the other. She rests in the
fulcrum, vigilant.

**Night is an open space which should not be
crossed alone.** Night is camouflage, night is risk;
shelter is the embankment a herd raises against
the wind.

I Saw You

I saw you, bounding over the shingle in the Summer dawn.
How typical of you to choose a hare, out there, solitary;
part Ariel, part Caliban, elusive, out of place;

heading from Dungeness B and a lighthouse lost in the fog;
past a vessel's skeleton, a collapsing slipway,
a string of black huts scattered along the road.

You came to forage for grave goods; beach-combing;
stricken fingers gathering driftwood, shaping a cenotaph
of rusty metal, mallow and tough sea holly.

Tar-black weatherboard blurs in the distance;
you turn your face to the wall.

A blue screen fills your sightless eyes;
sounds and sweet airs fade to silence.

Outside; the bounding hare, the endless horizon.

David Lewis

Lobster

that murky olive green or lustrous blue
turning bristling boiling furious pink
They say they scream; an angry swansong
quite a feat without a vocal chord
a shriek too quiet to pierce the heart

but how to kill a time machine
a million years have engineered
to roam at will, to shed a shell
grow stronger and more fertile till
a lobster pot spells curtains, crimson probably
to all that clawed complexity

I've seen them march on tiptoe
silent armies knowing where to go
the ocean floor their mating map
the silent depths' opacity no obstacle
they have more sense than us down there

up here we crack the coral shell
with special tools we scoop the flesh
we relish the un-kosher meat
expensive treats made rare by us
expanding waistlines round the world
deforesting the ocean floor

while we beach our basted bodies in the sun
an angry world is turning lobster red
the claws of boiling seas are snapping shut
a forest fire is headed for the shore
a barbecue inferno chases down the sand

meanwhile the lobsters go on dreaming
their unfathomable dreams

Davis Lewis

A Midsummer Night's Dream

Love songs spill from the forest brow,
the kind that keep me up at night—
if you would only teach me how
the love songs spill from the forest brow.
I wonder, do you fancy romance now?
I worry we won't get the lyrics right.
Love songs spill from the forest brow,
the kind that keep me up at night.

Chloe Hanks

The Forest

~~The forest edge breathed me in.~~
~~I think I feared it at first,~~
~~which might not surprise you;~~
~~it seemed hungry and empty and cold,~~
~~and I shivered against the harshness of it.~~
~~I bought myself a new coat.~~

~~I'd been daydreaming of the forest~~
~~for a while.~~ She visits me like a
ghost come to teach me a lesson.
Sometimes it would wash over me
whilst I watched him sleeping and I knew
the forest would take me, eventually.
I'd always have to leave.

The truth sometimes colours itself
in for you—
creeping across the pages of the books
you try to bury yourself in. Screaming
in vibrant greens, icy blues: you belong
to the forest and she belongs to you.

I get lost in the chasm of her eyes;
I was always going to end up in here.
Better men than you have tried to steer me.
Girls like me ache for the emptiness until
it comes and we wrap ourselves
from the branches.

The forest sings me lullabies and she
takes me for walks. She brings flowers;
but flowers die. Did you know that?
The thing I like most is that no one can get in.
She wraps me in an isolation that no prince
could slice his way through.

Chloe Hanks

Long Nights

She hasn't been letting me sleep lately,
she knows I'd leave her for you
in a heartbeat.

The spell is not quite broken
but desire is a powerful magic.
Part of me trusted you to break it,
did you know that?

I gave in to the forest a little while ago,
I made promises and blood pacts,
told myself I was worthy of that.
She hasn't forgiven me for getting into your car
and slipping your tongue into my mouth—
the forest doesn't allow.

She wakes me up at 4am and
makes me face up to it:
the rules of the trees, the make-believe.
We know when we take each other
in our arms that it ends here,
the lonely is our life partner
and the winter
our content.

She makes me replay
you leaving again.

And again.

Chloe Hanks

MOTHER

She fell to her dirty knees,
a supplicant,
crumbling upon the moss
in exhausted, broken prayer.

The blood in her lungs
was replaced with wet air
and she tasted the waiting forest,
expectant and patient.
Creaking leaves reached sunward
and the mud made its home
beneath her fingernails
as she dug down, deep,
scooping the dirt into her praying hands,
in desperate worship,
grinding it into her skin.

Bark broke through her skin,
kissed to life by lichen,
hair curled into ivy,
lips bloomed to blossom,
and petals fell
from her chestnut eyes
as she melted like spring dew
or winter snow,
drifted like an autumn fog
or a summer breeze.

The world had stolen her from herself,
a grand thief,
but now she runs
back to the earth,
back to her mother,
back home,
in ways they could only dream.

Georgie Broad

PROMETHEAN

Gods can burn, too.

Fire licks their flesh
as they hold in their marbled hands
a promise of danger
and a hope of redemption.

Flames burn like the bright chains will,
crackling, whispering, ripping,
fluttering like the wings of crows,
of angels,
as they tumble from the cradle of the heavens.
They dance,
the flames,
among earthly shadows
from whom their warmth was stolen,
pulled away and pulled apart.

Fire waits for no man, though,
burning through your meagre warnings.
That's what Gods are for,
To be bathed in your flames
And brought back from the dark.

Gods will burn, too.

Georgie Broad

Night Birds

Walking in the garden, pulling bluebells
through arthritic fingers,

you tell me about the dusk chorus, how some
birds sing their loudest as the sun beds down.

We can hear them getting ready,
drawing air through their bills

down into lungs the size
of spider heads, air sacs the

bellows that inflate, deflate,
as tympanums vibrate.

One solitary note comes, then another,
bound to meet in flight.

Bird words collide like
blind arms embracing.

This is what we ageing creatures do:
drive our voices into the world

ink the sky with sound,
as night moves over the bluebells

searching for its place to be born.

Flora Cruft

The Heartbeat of Trees

after Peter Wohlleben

My brother built a treehouse as a kid, fifty-foot up an old beech in the woods next to my big school, years before I learnt anything there. He coaxed me to climb it — the silver-grey bark was hard & slippy — I was a shaking leaf, like many boys in my brother's presence. He climbed ahead like a cat, not a leopard with its prey but with a nonchalant faith its kin would follow. I can't remember what was in the treehouse apart from a long-way-down-look.

At the big school next to the woods, I'd tell my classmates my brother built *'that'* — pointing to a branched sky. I'm sure no-one believed me but I now know that doesn't matter.

Twenty-odd years later, after he died, I searched for the treehouse and found remnants still hanging, my brother left in the arms of a trunk — *a place where important memories are kept*. I'm certain my brother carved hard into the bark and even though I couldn't recognise which, it was about a girl.

In 1860, the Brothers Grimm published a dictionary in which they told a tale of old Germanic characters etched into beech wood — *Buche* — pronounced in a similar way to book — *Buch* — where this story is. In it, I still remember how I shook like a 'quaking aspen' — *populus tremuloides* — whose flattened leaves tremble in light breeze.

Maybe I was reassured of my health & safety or medical care because our family doctor, Dr. Hafizullah — *remembrance of a god* — lived across the road. He also had three sons who were our friends. Faisal was my age, Anwar the age of my sister and I think she fancied him because he looked like Donny Osmond, but I'm not sure. What I do know is, my brother would have whispered a light breeze in his ear.

I don't recollect the name of the other son — a friend of my eldest brother who I don't really know anymore either, but his friend Robert also had a treehouse, in an oak tree — *with wood hard and resistant to weathering, just as families should be.* I only remember its plush carpet. Someone has long-since chopped it down.

A German word for true is *treu*, in the way memory often puts things the wrong way around, how this story takes me back to those woods next to my big school, where I pointed to the sky and was proud.

Simon Maddrell

dungeness

i.m. Derek Jarman

the driest body in england	but the inside
an isolation	full of
sagging shells	oozing
radiation in the bones	dog roses
bleached and skeletal	sea kale
leaves rotted	dried out
sickness blows through me	like tumbleweed

fucking like fairlight donkeys	more of a joy than bother
sex kittens still scamper in	my garden
gorse passion	red poppies splash
my body	the landscape
where it remains	rusting chains
a threaded necklace	water to gravel
hanging	dust to wind

Simon Maddrell

Wind

Those old, sighing gods.
The pollen-hustlers
and cloud-bringers.
The roof-tuggers and leaf-whisperers.

Each night-haunter and rain-charmer.

The dust-deliverers
and thunder-harbingers.
Widowmakers. Fret-givers.
Snowdrifters.

All of those rumoured
or half-remembered swirlers.
Reloaded rippers.
Appearing or disappearing at will.

Uncontainable and liminal mystics,
this enumeration of winds.
This roll call of all.

Each powerhouse.

Libby Hart

The Distance

we were all like satellites once —
little one, how you remind me.

after your bedtime, the moon is
a solitary stud pinned onto a darker blue,

the cool air strewn with whispered stars.
I could stay here all night, looking upwards,

on the edge of some uncharted land,
some sort of outcast purity up for grabs,

like a single lost glove temporarily freed
from its master's hand,

found by the wayside of a road; caught
amongst forget-me-nots.

Luciana Francis

Wanderlust

Something outside of me, of my body, of this house.
Something roaming beyond the eerily quiet,
dimly-lit suburban streets.

Something crawling proudly;
prodding its surroundings, sniffing.

Something that bleeds and heals.
Something dwelling fearlessly under the moon, full.
Something that seldom tires because it is free.

Something treading the ground
without the need to scar it, or to make it home.

Something licking its own wounds,
prowling along rivers — it is only a matter of time.

Something getting caught
by the nape of the neck, brought closer and fed.

Something with fur in its body, with sharp claws or beak.
Something elusive to daylight, to passers-by,
and the naked eye.

Something circling, hovering and then swooping;
with talons that grab and lift.

Something with fangs, and so close to the source
that its breath can fan the embers.
Something free from grammar.

Something in me that wishes to oblige
to the silent call in the cool night air.

Luciana Francis

Ode to the Mirror Carp

I.
Look! How they spin, fins vibrating and O-mouthed,
scales beating in a blood-rush.

Mother asks: have you ever heard a fish scream?
It's like a body rupturing, eating itself whole before re-entering the womb.

This is how girl becomes woman.

II.
There's a burning in their stomachs only death can cure.
Their hunger? Watch it rage, it's the only thing that draws fish out of water.

See their bodies pirouette for the last time,
they'll stop squirming soon.

This is how a woman lives.

III.
Mother reels them in.
I have her hands – I know, mine are just as impossible to hold.

Dinner will be served soon.
I open and close my mouth, and swim, and swim.

This is how we survive.

Nabeela Saghir

Awe

The codes that make   me   make   you
are 60 per cent   identical to   a   ripe   strawberry

70 per cent   to an   ear-shelled   slug.   All   atoms
are   99 per   cent   space.   A news feed   reminds me

life   is   like   a   dart of   kingfisher,
existence   is   the anagoge.   I   am   forged   from stardust

a galaxy of   particles   serendipitously   arranged.   You are
armed carbon   neurone   fire   and   lightning

shaping   the world with   the   gift of   will.
I am a cosmos   choosing to take   give   or share

an   idea   an   expression of love   so it   may   be
caught   like a   virus. We can be the curators of   kindness

the stars   clothed   in skin.

Nia Solomon

Ovulation

When I feel between my thighs
I'm as slick as a seal in water, wet
with an ache at my root. A bass note
of being woman not base, but natural
like a rising tide pulled to shore by the moon.
My womb counsels *remember the perfume,*
pine and juniper burning in the old huts, the red tents?
Stone circles call, sing back to me the old knowledge.
And I dream new stories.

Nia Solomon

Atlas in Regents Canal

I went to the canal and poured my spine
over the rail to see my shadow silhouette,
but instead I saw Atlas
holding up the sky within the murk.

Her hair she'd ripped out of her head.
The sky rested on the surface of the water
and the surface rested on her pitted skull.

I asked if she knew she was bearing the canal,
while the sky, slung above like an absurdity,
remained airborne. No, she had not known.

She climbed from the green and stood by me,
dripping watery time from her fists.
She asked if I knew who was holding the sky.
I didn't.

Rachel Lewis

Pond Scum

Trees bleed up the sky
like ink & I wonder

if there's a way to live without
getting your hands dirty.

O, to be
a pond skater,
the world
so small in
my stone-marked circle!

Clouds of copper
minnows, mosquitofish,

the looming shadow
of some unspoken

dread, & when
the sun retires

so too does he,
the water
left unstained,
leaving nothing
but me, braced

for ripples in the film.

Phoebe Kalid

Knot

In my family, grief is in the weather, when water
thickens over limestone and floods us, when hurt
closes in like heavy air and the turlough swells,
rippling out over county lines. My auntie tells me
how the swell came to her brother, how it put them
in a car going nowhere. The air rises in me as I hear her
tell it, water table fluctuates: these stories only arrive
once, shucked from a tender memory and prized
as they appear in my hands. I can see the water
in them, racing by the car, attempting
to outrun deluge. They drove for hours, no mind
of where, until they stopped in Sneem—*if ever there was
an end of the world, Sneem.* So remote it's named for a knot,
the last thing to tie us to land. Nothing there for them
but being somewhere else. She does not tell me
what they did or what was said, only that they stayed
until need turned them back. I watch the water
flow between us, mirror-sharp, and then disappear,
while I'm dammed in, thinking of Sneem.

Éadaoín Lynch

'Knot':
*Turlough – literally 'dry lake,' a feature of karstic limestone areas (such as The
Burren in North Clare), where apparent lakes will emerge overground after heavy
rains, with no natural surface outlet—principally filled by subterranean waters—and
disappear again when the water table rebalances.*

Huathe

ᚻ

Blowing through teeth of a drystone wall,
the gale, *gaoithe*, summons a sea behind it,
scraping rivulets from the land, making scraw
of the hawthorn. A gale is better than a blast,
a fairy wind, sudden and quick, compassed
by terrible quiet. But this screeching air
twists hawthorn askew in dense wiry
gnarls that crease the sky. Wind supplants
its branches, intersecting their upward
glance, a perfect three cross-roads.
Gaoithe is wise, teaching the briar
its name, *sceach gheal*, hiding thorns
beneath its blossoms. Fissures
in the wood appear with age,
wrinkles like scars, and do not die, even
when that scent is on its petals.

What sharp
ache brought someone to a fairy tree
and dare touch it, skin its skin,
pluck its fruit, tear its leaves?
Bound in to briars, pierced in the side
with hope, until the air was silent—petals
frozen in suspense, waiting for the wind.

Éadaoín Lynch

Huathe – the name of the Ogham symbol included with the text, which translates to 'H.'
It also means 'hawthorn.' - Gaoithe – Irish, 'winds,' with an etymological root in 'wise.' -
Sceach gheal – Irish, 'hawthorn.'

Hills In Scotland

What epic bones
hold up that hill-
Hearts hang at the bottom of
our throats,
beating a wilderness-
set loose from between the lungs.

Back horizontal from the waist
up the bent slope-
staring at rocks
mapping a broken path,
red-faced, falling on backsides
into the soft summit peat.
A white delivery van, glazed in rain,
moves feather-like on the road below.

A granite church damned by lichen and rot,
the
churchyard wall-
            the lambs by the yew tree.
Palette of oil-paint landscape,
low valley lochs.
Fog hesitating above an
isle in the distance.

To the wind we send back
our breath-
relearning the way that it usually flows.
The echoing volley not easily recaptured-
as we claw our fingers into
the earth
　　　　to stand.

Stephanie Powell

Moon song-

Imagine my womb,
as the moon-
          and
the closer I get to
my mid-thirties, the more you
astronauts come (*bouncing like fools*),
to stick in flags-
penetrate its craters,
kick up dust over my skin.

Though I don't know if I want a baby.
Though I don't know if I don't want a baby.

Imagine me: *not a planet, more of an archipelago,*
a guiltiness-   *some landmass malformed,*

felt at the root of each
cramp. At night woken by,
     angry muscles with tautness of pulled chicken wire-
knowing what is
coming but waiting
          a little longer, before
I empty out, wipe myself-
unoccupied again.

The moon a blushing claret,
my womb continues to
pulse as-
a third lung, living far deeper
than my chest,   *a distant, coal-fired moon, blood satellite.*

Stephanie Powell
                    42

Blood Pudding, Camping Trip

Where the boat rocks we grip
The sides, rails of metal slide
Under our palms.
I nurse handfuls of lake water,
Submerged skin like drowning paper.
The tide at our sides,
Nuzzling the fibro like a cat.

Where usually the sky could be
Described as open, an unending
Palm of cobalt blue, it bears the
Consistency of blood pudding,
The weighty suet and grain thrown
Up over its ceiling. Sunset burning
Like unpoetic pork fat under
Grey cloud.

Hills gather like the heads
Of school children, seated
Unevenly in rows, untrimmed.
In the morning we will plot the
shoreline, under meaty skies.
Waiting for a change in weather.
The soil like rusk, many times tread,
Cooked many times over by the sun.
A cold moon lingering.

Stephanie Powell

Negative capability

I have — a lack
where poems pool

a hollow
where words ring

better than any
thing

Moira Walsh

Survivor's Sonnet

For me

For those who don't know if the blood is theirs.
who have been cracked open, constellation by constellation.
kill your past. kill it dead, because
he drew and quartered your future, so
carve your body open. pour yourself on the pavement
and wait until it gets hot enough, then cook yourself alive
rise from it, let the birdsong rip your lies apart
because you are most dangerous at dawn.
scatter, scatter into a supernova.
when you think you're done,
when a smile doesn't split your lips, or if you're just fucking tired
that's when you will know you have survived.

Kayleigh Jayshree

Catching Raindrops - A Renga

leaves quiver
wind flirts with blossom ...
a curlew calls

    crow quills for drawing
    turkey feathers for fletching

red arrows
slash a wing commander's sky ...
a thousand necks crane

    catching raindrops
    on our tongues

despite the drizzle ...
Guy Fawkes winks as flames
tickle his collar

    it's easier to breathe
    nearer the floor

the ground trembles
saucers and plates rattle ...
grandma purls one

    waiting for a Victoria Line train
    to Seven Sisters

supporters chant ...
a police officer speaks to her watch
her mount nods

horseshoes made of iron
are more effective against goblins

aluminium ...
worn only once even by
race winner

no need to polish
a wooden spoon

sugar ...
ill advised medicine assistant
these days

I carry an umbrella
in case the wind changes

Haiku by Roger Noons
Couplets by Ros Woolner

Almost Infinity

A Peony blooms to almost infinity, unaware.
Ripples of uncountable petals, fluttering with softness, spilling over
seams.
      She sprawls proudly.

A Fawn shyly nuzzles the ground, stubbled fur against soaked leaves.
She seeks the instinctual comfort of fullness.
      She does not need to earn it.

A Jackdaw caws coarsely for intimacy.
He nests, unscathed by reproach, whether he receives it or not.
      He does not feel shame.

A wood cherishes its need to grow.

You wrap, conceal and betray your stomach,
and apologise for existence.

Ella Squire

39 days

I miss you with my throat.
Each fibre and nerve flossing my voice box
Until it ignites

Yet - wordless. My mouth should have forgotten you, the way your
name curled around my tongue when you moved in me.
Ten days for tastebuds to regenerate, yet 22 days later I can still feel
your lips
And the way they opened and closed with rattled finality.

Someone else kissed me on Saturday.
I'd felt them before, but this time they felt rough, forced and firm
Like a head torch into my skull.
Could he feel the remnants of you in my strained tonsils, cheeks and
chest? What was left?

Where will I feel you last?

Google claims I only have 17 days left before every single cell of my skin
is a stranger to you.

Ella Squire

After the Fall

a whole swarm of butterflies at the bottom of the pit
fall in line like sparrows and dance their way
around fish and sea to fill up the whole
volume of their container like a gas, like helium
lifting a weight with ease that slumped
heavy for so long under the chaos

fireworks light up the inside of a box and
push at its edges, expanding, giving more and more
space to plant the bulbs and seeds and trees
that give us shade and colour and life

oh, the simplicity of looking at a face
every day and feeling the sand come
back together with each motion of the chest,
pushing and pulling like the dawn waves

J. Daniel West

Baptism

The friction of the lighter wheel scrapes like a stiletto heel
The spikes grind round and I can feel them dig into my thumb
I twitch with zeal, I drop and kneel. The sermon has begun

A gentle hum of metered breathing as the embers start their teething
The sodden rag slumps damp in grieving bundled on the floor
Start perceiving God, believing He called for this encore

The air still tastes of gasoline as smaller flames come into being
I sit and watch, I'm calm, serene, my hand no longer shakes
Soon be seen my conscience clean absolved of my mistakes

Brick and mortar, slow to burn, patiently it waits its turn,
Listens to the wood beams yearn with aching cracks of pain
Soon to learn the stomach churning touch of the arcane

Moving to the virgin light standing out against the night
I heed the call of holy rite deep within my soul
And at the sight my shards unite, my parts become a whole

Red and yellow spark with flare and crackle in the blackened air
Hypnotised, I simply stare and marvel at God's beauty
With Him I share this cleansing prayer, this sacramental duty

The hymn picks up with burning chords, takes me as it rises towards
The cradle of my waiting Lord awakened by the voice
My just reward of being adored gives reason to rejoice

See the flame become a fire, tongues that reach up ever higher
Chant the hymnal cry of choir and all my sins are purged
Before the pyre, the dancing spire of my luminated church

Stepping back I stare in wonder as the building's torn asunder,
Bellows loud with ripping thunder rising from the earth
Brick and lumber collapsing under the process of rebirth

I've prayed so many times before but now I cannot be so sure
I have it in me anymore to top my magnum opus
I kneel before Him and implore Him, meek and tired and hopeless

I hear the whispers calling me ever more enthralling, He
Pulls me in, I'm falling. Feel the blisters on my skin
Appallingly I'm crawling free from every ounce of sin

J. Daniel West

While Wearing Sunglasses the Sun Kind of Looks like the Moon

and poets always write about the moon
at one time or another   that
deity extreme   whorshippable golfball shot too far
from the bunker of downtoearth realism

where the sun   mighty and allpowerful
is a lightbulb of daytoday duties   of bank statement
woes and little treat pleasures   the
dazzling nuisance of fortunes forgiven

for the sake of survival   the day is a bully
the body bruised by the *musts* and *have tos*   slips
into the bathtub at night   settles into
the darkness the way a shark settles into the ocean

then stops

sinks

Dale Booton

Hatchling

send me ur pix i will return after   and you did
salty-eyed   soft-lipped   innocent
like a newly hatched chick looking out
at the world for the first time   you wanted flight
but did not yet understand the rhythm
of your own wings   you wanted height
but couldn't bear to look down   held your feathers
like a blanket you wanted
someone else to weave   I tried
nursed you with cocktails and chips then
walked you back to your nest   you told me
of your migration   of how in summer
you'll sing the song of my hands
of the touch you said tasted something like freedom

Dale Booton

We Fuck Like The First Time

we fuck like the first time   restless groaning

in days I will watch your comet
from the road side
try to follow
its trail
only to fall into
a black hole

we wake my neighbours   headboard to the wall

in weeks you will travel
beyond my orbit
across the patchworked sky
of bitten pillows
set alight
like invading stars

we come together   one inside one out

in years I will think of the bed
the moonsweat
of skin cratered by fingers
where the universe
was made of
us

Dale Booton

Destroying Angel*

I come to thee veiled ,
I come to thee gleaming
of gill and membrane.

How I be made so?
all alone in this dim church
of oak cloister.

I be a shared self,
born out of root coppice
and soil forest tracing,

of underworld dark.
I felt, felted, fruited,
followed rainwater seam

until up I pushed,
shaped and stiffened
my milky birth,

pearled into this light.
Now I float above my stalk
like a vision.

Kneel.
Take me inside you
and we shall be married,

then I shall become your bride.
Later, deep within, I trail my broken gown
towards your heart.

The Destroying Angel (Amanita Virosa) is a deadly fungus for which there is no antidote. Symptoms do not appear for 4-5 hours by which time it is too late.

Louise Warren

Blue

You don't talk about the chip in the brick anymore.
The wisteria holds the wall, like you inside my coat
on the days that I conspired with the wind to bring
you closer to me. The leaves have been dancing in
the heavy breathing of the patio, swaying in the breeze,
as indecisive as the wagtails that have been landing
on the fence, staring at the bird feeder with equal
measures trepidation and temptation in their gaze.
They never hesitate like this with the grass seed.

You made me put a bird house up on the back fence
and I swore it was stupid until two blue tits came
to look around the property It's open plan
with a nice garden, but you have to bring your
own bedding. We watch them come and go,
we know the magic of home building, we know.

The buds on the golden birch have started creeping
out of springtime, just when we had accepted
it's passing, it is laughing from the corner of the
garden, "I'm not the orange tree that you left
out through the winter you know".

You don't talk about the chip in the wall anymore,
imperfections go missing in the pirouette
of contentment. When smoke climbs to reach
the clouds, it may slip from sight but it doesn't
become water and ice. You don't look past blemishes
lightly, but I know how you've stood by my me
so I know what it means when the damaged wall
no longer causes stress. We are home, here.

I wave to the neighbour out of the back window
she, looking through the circular hole
in her wooden haven, sings her morning song
I drain the last of the coffee, and survey
the in between. You catch me looking for growth
and tell me it is on this side of the glass.

Casey Bailey

Dry

I have been me for nearly as long
as I wasn't, now. I was two hands
wringing blood from road signs,
spilling into the echoes of voices
that promised family and delivered
oak/pine/mahogany. Open earth,
and faces dried by mothers' tears

still hold onto the back of my neck
as I look at the same sky that escaped
me then. Orion's Belt is the line
in the sand, but life is not the beach
they sold us. I will walk that road
again, speaking to the street lights
until the morning takes you back.

Casey Bailey

Japanese Knotwood

Bamboo-like stems, leaves protruding
above the thicket. Judgemental.
Spreading like news of an invasion
strangling what has always been here.

One of the most invasive non-native species,
stands here in the garden of a coloniser,
like karma on a postcard, like bloodstains
on old money. Bloodstains on all money

It's dangerous because it can outcompete
the native flora, grows through concrete
crumbling structures that could bring
down buildings and erode river banks.

Even severed and dismantled beyond trace
they persist, rooted so deeply into landscape
that was never theirs. Here, in a garden
of a coloniser they wreak havoc.

Casey Bailey

A Prophecy

these long thigh-bones will make
    cudgels for a hunter

my ribs a xylophone
    tuned for a ritual dance

the knucklebones will entertain
    soldiers gambling under a hanged man

my hide will bind a bible
    for a blind soothsayer

whose hands will scan the chapters
    for clues to each new disaster

my split skull will serve
    as drinking-bowl for a king in exile

this flesh will feed crows
    and enrich a patch of land

where an acorn will put down a root
    and lift two leaves into the light

Ama Bolton

Water From The Well

I roll out of bed into a summer's morning
  set off with the sun rising behind me
    half a hazy moon high in the sky

walk under jasmine and Magnolia grandiflora
  where a blackbird practices today's variations
    and white poplar flashes silverback leaves

wild oats quiver in the verge
  mallow burdock hogweed ragwort
    elderberries hard and green

after the road-sign on the parish boundary
  a scatter of pale feathers
    woodpigeon wry-necked under a lilac hedge

at the spring at Littlewell descend three steps
  fill the bottle with a gallon of fresh water
    filtered through limestone for a thousand years

trudge homeward sun in my eyes
  pick up a pint glass white plastic fork
    disposable mask squashed cola bottle

black vinyl glove McDonald's cardboard cup
　　ants come single file up through the straw
　　　　onto fingers and wrist

put the glass on the pub doorstep
　　and the rest in a builder's skip
　　　　knowing that nothing is disposable

Ama Bolton

Learning to Run With Scissors

Beholden to the tradition of salting wounds on anniversaries. I become something of an expert on both techniques to prolong life expectancy & on drowning. I am starting to cultivate bone in place of memories. To develop flood defences rather than coping strategies. To allow all the lies I tell myself to keep the sea at bay to take root. I'm hoping it will save us, knowing it won't. I have gained a taste for the measuring of grief - a tongue whose wound I am fluent in. I'm fraught with knowledge. Beset by information. Burdened by forgetting. I wasn't to know there would be a time I would wish to be overwhelmed. Observing the remnants of sowing season peels back the day from its wreckage & there's no reason for the limits we place on ourselves hoping to be far better than we are. No reason the sea should grow just because we planted it in our torsos hoping to become islands. No reason our last monument to forgetting has become something of a celebrity in my absence. But it has. So, we proselytise the notion our history should dictate how we act in context of those to come after. It's an assurance we tell the grieving I have little time for.

Sam J. Grudgings

Stealing Flowers From Other People's Gardens

the first, a nasturtium –
plucked from the green waste
a searing orange star
asleep and aflame
extinguished on an unwashed tongue

lavender follows – burning husks
of last warmth a hundred bees
and a final sun-slant slinking
across the poppies' glass
red splinters slung towards the drain

I leave a scattered mass of dahlias
violent shafts of bitter light in my wake
petals gesturing their theft

I do not touch the foxgloves

walking home I clutch a sticky victory
translucent, clinging and summer-slicked
a mourning cradle
creased and darkening in my arms
for nothing
– no vase, or palm or pressing
until each petal tears
like crepe –

just a having feeling
shaming and delicious
plucked before the deadheading
in the dusk of another day
without a garden of my own.

Laura Jayne

The Gardener Thinks Of Touch

brushed earth, cool fingers stretch
to clip the yarrow Achilles pressed
against each wound, skin with skin
and a slip of leaves between that touch –

touch and Daphne is running
turning laurel already, bark and bitter
wet taste
and Hyacinthus struck is falling
long into Apollo's arms
purpled but unbruised
a larkspur in a lover's shade

again and again
tender bodies lined in fresh vellum
stretch taut, lingered on by a longing sun
leaning steady into the next wait

the gardener and her wettened knees
harvest galingale
tongues of fern
young heads of yarrow
palms of velvet sage
the knife pressed close - a clean cut -
the early hour turns the spade
no transformation
just fingers pressing into seeping earth
matching shape to greener shape.

Laura Jayne

Mock The Lads But Also Love Them

How, once, they were just two rural kids
with bowl-cuts, playing games of Army,
falling, like ash, into empty flowerbeds,
slowly removing the foil from his uncle's
Falklands rations, taste of dusty chocolate
and the hard metal of cycling in the rain.
And then the change: new sports jackets,
white, smeared with thumbprints of hash.
How they split apart like a bar of hot resin,
one turning silent, smoking joints in bed,
watching Trois couleurs: Bleu, the other
diving deep into the canals of adulthood,
on his tongue and lips, the taste of skin.
One travels to Amsterdam in the spring,
on a pilgrimage, makes priestly gestures
to a map of the city's weed cafés, finds
a nice hotel and goes to sleep. The other
never sleeps, but sings in autumn flames,
sails on star-lit tarmac, a vision: his body
on a barge through water dark as a lantern.

Will Pittam

Drum Lessons

First we learned the rudiments: single-strokes
and paradiddles, and how impossible it seemed,
back then, to play those lightning double-strokes.
In awe, we watched a tape of Tony Royster Jr,
his sticks transformed into a haze, a smoke.
Just like you did. Puff, and you were gone.
Your death was like a solo, a final flourish.
We liked that style. Bone-shattering. Buddy Rich.
But then, in the rehearsal rooms of Stoke-on-Trent,
where I played grinding punk and metal blast-beats,
I found this ghost of gentleness. The lead singer
of one of those bands was a librarian, his screaming
an extension of that gentle dark, the hush of pages
merely amplified. You might have been there, lying
cherubic on that snot-green sofa, exhaling into the cloud
of smoke and perspiration. Lager cans as ash trays.
Even that dank, stained room was soft as a meadow.
Even the drop-D, chug-chug chords were harp-like.
It felt like you were there with me as I got better,
trying to play with grace, I guess, with tenderness,
watching Papa Joe Jones, a drummer with a solo
that starts with a gaze, a smile, and hardly builds
beyond the whisper of his sticks against the snare.
I've come to think, now, that this is the way to play:
As close as possible to silence. Somehow it summons life.
Like the air, the sky, when I've come back to the village –
especially in summer – and the road where you lay.

Will Pittam

You Lined Our Room With Lanterns

A different flame filled each jar –
the red you plucked from a cherry tree,
blue scooped from the stream,
yellow sunlight stolen from the gaps
between trees.

Every night you locked our door,
I was grateful for their
swirling glows –

the heavy green across my covers,
the glassy orange of a monarch's wing
floating up one wall.
I thought
maybe this is what home feels like

until I noticed
the smallest lantern –
a snowberry orb
open-mouth-scream-shaped
under a tightly screwed lid.

Emilie Lauren Jones

Today I Wandered To The Lighthouse
Inspired by Virginia Woolf

I stood among the shale, studying the small forms
my hands had scooped from the shoreline –
abandoned spiral cones, empty cinnamon swirl shells –
a Mrs Dalloway style house party of minerals.
I knew they belonged to the beach, but I must confess,
I slipped them into my dress pocket before climbing the stone steps.
From this higher point I took in the panorama of blue eternity –
waves turning themselves over like pages of a diary.

I wish I could invite you to stand there with me,
alongside a flutter of sparrows whispering *'fáros'*,
our words leaving our lips in trickles of consciousness,
submerged in sunlight and stories, reflecting
on reflections, as only outsiders do.
Miss V, I would tell you tales of hashtags and metoo,
and how Anonymous is finally finding her names.

Emilie Lauren Jones

Fáros – the Greek pronunciation of 'lighthouse'.

Postcards From The Water's Edge

Wind has poured those thorns
into an unseen mould of air –
they are old women crouched
hugging their sacks of stones
that they cannot let go –
their roots cling into rock,
they are weighted by memories
heavier than themselves

Raindrops love the tall lilies;
they cannot not bear to fall.
So water pearls your hair, your skin,
and cannot bear to fall

Slick sand's silvered mirror reflects sky –
pounding waves fill ear's shell drum tight
so there's not a grain of room
for any other sound,
for any other thought

Once you are inside the shell,
in the deep heart of a white shell,
where you may be entirely private,
how beautiful the sun is,
filtered through those white walls

Shell woman has shattered again
into splinters of white light
cupped in the bowl of a black sea;
she'll reform smooth,
flawless as an egg
that does not need to hatch

And I'm going out to meet her
with the ebbing tide,
tide that has tattooed my skin
with rivulets running,
braiding into estuaries,
into roots of hawthorns;
I'm going out to meet her
with this tide

Sarah Dale

Wild Hunt

Cry wreck! Cry havoc!
Wild hunt's riding high tonight
to wrack and ruin, and I,
I've had enough of making and mending,
I'm in this storm
sliding my knife under trees,
driving my fingers into rotten concrete
bringing bridges down
with all their flailing cargo,
matchsticking boats to flotsam,
rivering roads with flood,
and all, all, petty artifices
of safety, of control, of order
mean nothing to me now –
let all this dry world drown,
let all be washed away,
dissolved away to nothing;
Cry wreck! Cry havoc!

Sarah Dale

Vappu

Tonight
on Walpurgis night,
witch's night, Vappu,

the fox will leave
this snowy mountain
to burrow a new home.

In his place,
at the highest peak,
all of us shall gather

and under the light of Freya
build a fire
and give to it our winters.

We shall dance ourselves
into the mountainside,
our feet welcome to ash

and if our fire dies
then we shall drink and wait
for the power of a thunders flash.

Before the morn we'll leave an offering
of buttered bread with honey;
it'll keep the phantom hounds tame

and as the sun returns
we'll join hands and jump through
to the other side of the flame.

Bradley Blue

Waterswallows

I have left the washing line   the garden tomatoes
pleading like children with my knees   for water
for less shade   for more shade   feed

I have left my laptop sleeping.   my handbag
curled like a hedgehog   in the bottom drawer
dreaming of loose coins   Trebor   and lipsticks

I love the catkins   the startled calves   the storm of cans
and glass on bin day   but also this silence.
I leave my life on the stones   with my socks

and the water accepts my clumsy.   The shy way
I knee by knee go in   to the quarry
all angles and stumbling.   The water admits me

like a mother.   like a lover.
like the usher in the spot-lit   entrance of a theatre.
I mill the splinters of light   with my fingers.

My heart is a moon.   It pulls all the blood
to my centre. I hang   in the blue. In the far.
I used to be star -   I remember -

Cheryl Pearson

78

Oxygen

Think of a million mouths pursed into an O
and inhaling together, one giant in-suck.

Forget that dream where you always wake
gasping and clutching at your throat.

Think of bubbles rising in a lake –
like them we must release ourselves towards air.

Now that the cool has come, the edges
have softened in the garden a little, our wren

is at ease with herself and we of late
have taken to sitting out, fanning ourselves

and watching the deepening shadows.
There is an art to this – to breathing easy;

half lung-capacity and half blind faith
that the next breath will come,

that we will not flounder and choke
on our filthy emissions, on sticky particulates,

that we will, somehow, mostly, get it right.

Not unlike like that river fish, the pike,
who lords it over his river underlings,

his green slime-shimmer stalled among the weeds,
his razor- jaws, so cruel, so cannibal,

his habit, or if you like, his trick
of flicking his prey to swallow it head first,

and whole, and live.
How he only rarely misjudges, gags,

thrashes a little, turns belly up and dies.

Róisín Tierney

Acknowledgements

This anthology would not have been possible without the exceptional poets and their stunning responses to the theme. Huge thanks to all of our published poets, and also to everyone who submitted their work during our open window. The standard of poems we received was extraordinary and I am very grateful to have read them. I truly have discovered some of my favourite poets in the making of this anthology!

Thank you to Lexia Tomlinson, without her assistance in reading and selecting submissions, I would still be knee-deep in papers to this day! Thank you for your insight, wisdom, and outstanding motivational energy. You are an inspiration in all that you do. Special thanks to our brilliant Intern Konnie Colton, for always going above and beyond in any task and for being an integral part of this project coming together.

Thank you to Mike Gates from Kingate Press for the patience, the guidance throughout production, and for truly excellent service. Particular mention to Floyd the dog who sat in on our meetings, and who is a very good boy.

Thank you especially to my dad Kerst Ward, who was on hand to assist with any and all of my design queries, and didn't disown me when I jammed his home printer printing the submissions shortlist.... nor when I used all of the ink... and paper.

Thank you to Beetfreaks and the FUEL funding programme, which facilitated much of this to take place, and allowed Fawn Press to create opportunities such as our internship programme. Thanks go also to Jamil Shabir and Bootcamp Media, whose kind donation facilitated the employment of a BSL interpreter for our live launch events.

Last but certainly not least thank you, dear Reader, for joining us in this journey!

Scarlett Ward-Bennett
Founder & Editor

About Fawn Press

Founded in 2021, Fawn Press aims to publish beautiful books of exceptional poetry, as we believe that poetry has the power to change lives through that transcendental connection between writer and reader. Storytelling lies at the very soul of our experience as human beings, connecting us since the dawn of time. We hope to be a platform that welcomes all writers, rejecting elitist and pompous attitudes to publishing in favour of an inclusive approach, whilst maintaining a high quality of writing that transports, excites and inspires.

"Poetry that takes you by the hand and leads you into the woods"

Fawn Press emerged from a passionate love of books and literature, as well as the recognition that the world needs more platforms for new and under-represented poets. It was born from the knot of the Midlands; Staffordshire. We hope to work closely with our Writers to become a home to high-quality publications, as we believe that the integral element sitting at the core of poetry, is the melody that sings to the reader.

FAWN PRESS